> The measure of TRUST that we put in a man or a woman will not determine the cost of BETRAYAL. It is the thin line between LOVE and HATE that measures whether one is willing to betray at all!
>
> ~~sdm~~ Jeremiah 17:9

TRUST RECOVERY SERIES

Self-Help Workbook

Session [I] ~ What You DID & Didn't SAY

Copyright © 2016 ~ by Dr. Sandy D. Murphy

P.O. Box 15211 ~ Humble, Texas 77347

(832) 303-2451 OR (281)372-0037
Email: betterfamily3@gmail.com
Website: www.buildbetterfamilies.webs.com
Cover Vision, Layout, & Interior design by:
Dr. Sandy D. Murphy

ISBN: 978-0692722633

Printed in the United States of America

ALL RIGHTS RESERVED

Unless otherwise noted, all Scriptures are quoted from the King James Version of the Bible. However, the Amplified or NIV Versions of the Bible will also be used to provide special emphasis where needed for more clarity. This book or parts thereof may not be reproduced in any form, stored in retrieval system or transmitted in any form by any means: electronic, mechanical, photocopy, recording or otherwise, without prior written permission of the publisher, except as provided by United States of America copyright law. *Before you copy any part of this book, please "Just ask me, I am willing to work with anyone; if you would only ask me." Thank you.*

Message To First Time Readers

If by chance you are a first time reader of my writing style, let me first say thank you for your interest. I find it very necessary to inform every reader that if by chance you are a grammar major, editor, or book critic and you should find some grammar errors, misspelled words, or sentences that don't make sense to you, it's all on purpose. *Just kidding!* But yes, you just might find some grammar errors in this book and prayerfully I will catch them soon. However, until I do this, either notify me or just simply pray with me about it. Dr. Murphy's email: eladysons@gmail.com. Thanks.

SEE DETAILS ON LAST PAGE HOW TO INSTANTLY RECEIVE YOUR FREE eBook by Dr. Murphy

Dr. Sandy D. Murphy

DEDICATION & APPRECIATION

To My "Abba" **Thank you for loving, forgiving, saving, anointing, and *breaking* me to become**

YOUR *purpose driven* PREACHER-WOMAN

I am grateful to Dr. Serena Washington for her kind support in assisting me with the publication of this Workbook. I am also grateful to all those who sowed into this publication; and for reading and sharing of my Books over the years. May God bless you all abundantly for your generous contributions.

I'M NO LONGER A VICTIM!
©*Copyright Dr. Sandy Murphy 6/06*

We can only imagine **the pain of the battered, raped, and abused**

We can only imagine the oppression, depression, and thoughts of suicide from emotional torment

We can only imagine the evil forces of terror and fear from gang violence and stalking

We can only imagine the deep hole in ones heart from the loss of a loved one, and the lingering spirit of grief

We can only imagine the fear, confusion, hurt, and shame of an innocent child who suffered molestation, incest, or abduction, from spirits of perversion and lust

We can only imagine the torment and fear of someone facing murder by the hands of those they loved or thought they could trust

Yes ..... *We can only imagine* the pain, sorrows of death, violence, and terrors of ungodly men

Yet, we still ponder in our hearts questions of ...why? who? and when?

But no matter what our answers may be, the fact will always remain the same. It was the ungodly that preyed upon every victim!

But in their distress they called upon the Lord and He heard their voices out of His temple, and their cry came before Him, yes directly into His ears!

Glory to God, They Are No Longer Victims! But Victors!

For out of His temple He came quickly as He rode upon a cherubim He sent out his arrows, shot out lightening, confused, and subdued them!

Yes...It was the Lord God Almighty who enlightened their darkness and girded them with strength for the battle against violent men

What manner of man is this that He would be mindful of them!

He is their Lord and shield...... Mighty in battle!

For by Him, some have conquered death and leaped over the walls of shame and un-forgiveness

And through the power of His love, He delivered them from the clutches of sin and death

Let the God of their salvation be exalted with thanksgiving and praise

Let the heavens and the earth declare His glory!

For the Lord has lifted their heads above their enemies; and even people who they don't know shall respect and serve them

Glory to God for the GREAT deliverance and mercy He has given to His anointed ones

They Are No Longer Victims....   *They Are Victorious!*

Dr. Sandy D. Murphy

Welcome to Dr. Murphy's TRICS Sessions. TRICS stands for TRUST RECOVERY *Inner-healing Counseling Series*. TRICS is an Inner-healing Counseling Self-help Session Workbook specifically designed to help you deal with the *"silent betrayal echoes"* of your past or present that often suddenly *"wake-up"* persistent unwanted painful and moody mindsets.

TRICS is a great Self-help Session that will assist you with a wide range of reoccurring emotional problems. You can use this Workbook in a number of ways: as a Group Facilitator Guide for a class/workshop, and as part of individual or self-help therapy. Dr. Murphy is hopeful that your experience with this Session will help you to discover how you may best face and release your silent pain in a way that will nourish your deepest capacity for inner-healing and wholeness. One must learn to recognize the difference between freedom and condemnation. Liberty and not bondage is the Lord's heritage for His children. The question is: *Which one are you enjoying?*

Ps. 23:3 tells us that Jesus restores our souls by leading us into the paths of righteousness away from the paths of destruction, which we have either chosen for ourselves or have been lured into by the agents of the enemy; such as spirits of Jezebel, Absalom, Miriam, dream killers, emotional/physical abusers, or others seeking to divert us from the paths of God. *There is a way that seemeth right unto a man, but the end thereof are the ways of death. Prov. 14:1.* Millions of victims/survivors have not been able to feel whole due to the devastating memories of their painful past or present oppressive relationships. Their souls are *fragmented* and held captive to the painful voices or evil deeds from what someone SAID or DID. I encourage you to pray the prayer below to *call back* and speak healing to your fragmented soul.

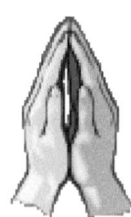 # Let us pray.....

Father, in the Name of Jesus I come today to repent for all the sins and iniquities that so easily beset me. I am making a decision today to break all unrighteous authority, manipulation, or control exercised over me. I renounce all unrighteous covenants; I loose myself from all unrighteous soul-ties and from every form of bondage of my soul or body to satan. In Jesus Name, I command every portion of my soul that has been fragmented, torn or broken to come back into its proper place; to be healed; every piece of my heart to be returned; my soul to be restored and every bondage or related soul-ties from my abuse to be completely broken. Lord, now I ask you to heal my heart and to guard it by Your power and Your love, and to keep my heart, mind, body, and soul through Christ Jesus. I offer my body as a living sacrifice to the Lord and I choose to walk in holiness. Through the power of the Blood and love of Jesus, I declare that I am free. *In Jesus' Name! Amen*

CONGRATULATIONS!

YOU HAVE JUST MADE YOUR FIRST STEP TOWARD HEALING

Whether you wish to believe it or not, there is *"hope"* for your past or present day situation. Before you begin to read this book please take a moment to silently pray and believe God for your healing. Then go and get a mirror and take a look at yourself. As you begin to look, take a serious in-depth look at the true person *"inside"* that reflects back at you even when you don't want him or her to. You know the person that is "hidden inside" of you who no one truly knows except you and God Almighty! It's an ugly and sad picture Hugh? I know how you feel because I too once had to face that same ugly and painful backlash of my past until I found the strength to fight the nightmare head-on with the naked TRUTH!

Dr. Sandy D. Murphy

This Workbook is designed to serve as a self-help, inner-healing and intervention guide for women, men, and teens who may be "suffering in silence" as a result of betrayal, disloyalty, or bullying.

When you finish this Workbook, please don't just put it away somewhere to catch dust. Instead, give it as a gift of life for *"Hope in Telling"* to someone you may know who too could be "suffering in silence" from this ever growing soul-robbing epidemic: BETRAYAL!

THIS WORKBOOK IS "HOPEFUL" INNER-HEALING FOR:

PERSON [who receives] NAME:

_____

Presented by [NAME]:

_____

MONTH_____ **DAY**_____ **YEAR**_____

Personal Message **by person who gave the Workbook:**

_____
_____
_____
_____
_____
_____
_____
_____
_____
_____
_____
_____
_____

Hope Journal Celebration Page!

In the space provided below, take a moment and write out any words of joy and excitement about your journey towards INNER-HEALING and freedom from the SECRET chains of SILENCE!

_____
_____
_____
_____
_____
_____
_____
_____
_____
_____
_____
_____
_____
_____
_____
_____
_____
_____
_____
_____
_____
_____
_____

Dr. Sandy D. Murphy

INTRODUCTION
I thought you were my Friend!
Psalms 55:11-14

I consider this Session a *"healing-companion workbook"* to my Session with Sandy book, *Why I Can't Trust You*. This Workbook was spiritually impregnated for me to deliver last year; but I was facing so many life-challenges, I wasn't sure if God wanted it back then. But for such a time as this with so much blood-shed from the lack of communication, miscommunication, and worst of all non-verbal communication continues to cause aggressive behavior. Millions of angry survivors of *"Betrayal Trauma"* quickly find themselves reacting from their "silent body pain" to the point of self-destruction or they tend to inflict harm to others. Any Believer can attest that the pain of betrayal from the Household of faith is one that cuts deeper than words can explain! To me, church-house betrayal feels like a part of you have been cut away and stuffed down somewhere deep inside" of your soul. This ugly "thing" hidden inside of you soon begins to feel like a big sore left alone uncared for to "weep" daily as it bleeds out the ugly pain of your past until gradually it begins to "rot" away at your conscious and soul. In Matthew 12:25 Jesus gave a principle about how a House divided against itself cannot stand. And even among relationships, this means that a team divided against itself by jealousy, envy, and competition will not stand.

Once we gain knowledge of the evil fruit from this spirit that lingers in our lives, in the church, in our relationships, or in our businesses, we can prepare ourselves so that we don't become victims; nor will we be used by it. But, if you find yourself being attacked by this spirit, glory to God for He is full of mercy and grace! There is forgiveness, inner-healing, and there is deliverance. All across America today and among the Body of Believers, there is a great need for a restoration of TRUST. Though I have suffered much as a child from Betrayal Trauma, I can still love and I will never lose hope or my joy! Psalms 119:71 have taught me that it is good for me that I have been afflicted that I might learn His statutes. Through God's grace I can rejoice for the strength that He has given me to help those who are "silently suffering" from this life-controlling generational curse.

Disloyalty and betrayal is ungodly and it is not the nature of Christ. God builds on TRUST in a covenant family community. If you cannot trust those around you, will not be able to build anything that will last. We need to spiritually RECOVER to be able to TRUST one another again through the love of God for all mankind.

We might as well face it, we are in a spiritual battle whether we care to admit it or not. Everyone is searching for answers, for inner peace and contentment, but precious few find lasting relief from the "silent rage" of betrayal and bondage from within. It is my prayer that what is presented in this Workbook will open the doors of light, hope, deliverance, and "inner-healing" for victims who are being held captive by the clutches of deception and betrayal.

Be glorified through this Abba!

Dr. Sandy D. Murphy

WHAT IS BETRAYAL TRAUMA?

Betrayal Trauma refers to the damage that is caused when someone experiences a betrayal in their primary relationship that damages the trust, safety and security of the bond they have with their partner.

The way that we bond to our mates is a profound puzzle. We are only starting to understand what happens inside the chemistry of our brains and bodies as we couple up and the two become one. What we do know is that in this mysterious bonding, we actually start to physically operate as one biological organism. "Numerous studies show that once we become attached to someone, the two of us form one physiological unit [soul-tie]. Our partner regulates our blood pressure, our heart rate, our breathing and the levels of hormones in our blood."

As we bond with our partners, through intertwining our lives, having children together and creating memories, we become more and more interdependent with one another. This is not codependency. This is healthy, normal, mutual emotional attachment or dependency. It is what makes relationships beautiful and sought after. We all want this special someone to attach to and intermingle our lives with.

[continued]

In fact, attachment researchers, talk about the paradox of attachment, "The more effectively dependent people are on one another, the more independent and daring they become."

So the better our relationships are in terms of providing us with a sense of, "I can depend on you" the more we are able to move fully into the rest of our lives, face insecurity and take risks. In this way our relationships provide us with a secure base from which we operate.

If it is true that when we attach to someone healthy and functional, it feels good and provides a sense of security, grounding, safety and wholeness, then the opposite is also true. When that attachment is breached or damaged it can affect our physical, mental, emotional and spiritual health in teeth-rattling ways. Instead of grounding us, it puts us in free fall. Instead of security we experience fear. Because our partner has caused us such deep pain, they now feel like a threat to our well-being rather than a source of comfort and rest. Sue Johnson, the founder of Emotionally Focused Therapy for Couples says that betrayal traumas, "overwhelm coping capacities and define *the...relationship*, as a source of danger rather than a safe haven in times of stress."

When that special someone that we have bonded with betrays us, it messes us up because all of a sudden the person who is our 'secure base' in the world has caused us untold pain and robbed us of our sense of safety.

By: Levine and Heller, 2012.

WHY ANOTHER MESSAGE ON TRUST?

Dr. Murphy has already written one Book describing the issues of TRUST for a wide audience. The **Why I Can't Trust You Book**; and this Workbook will complement each other; it is very helpful to use them both in order to effectively process your Trust Recovery.

If you have not read Why I Can't Trust You, you may find it a useful general introduction to the TRIC Session. It gives a lot of background details that might be particularly helpful if you are using this Workbook on your own, as a tool for self-help.

If you have read Why I Can't Trust You, this Workbook will give you all the additional tools and details practical guidance you need to take yourself through the TRIC Sessions.

Did You Know......

The patterns of mind that keeps people trapped in emotional suffering are fundamentally the same patterns of mind that stand between all of us and the flowering of our potential for a more deeply satisfying way of being.

WHY A WORKBOOK?

The backlash of Betrayal Trauma affects people in many ways. People's unique traits affect how they experience trauma. Some people experience significant distress following a traumatic event, while others seem to cope effectively with all sorts of painful and difficult circumstances. So, what distinguishes one person from another? The concepts of vulnerability and resilience help to explain these difference.

Vulnerability
If people already have a certain challenge in their lives, they may be more vulnerable to distress and more likely to develop long-term difficulties.

Resilience
People who cope effectively with distress are characterized as resilient. Resilient people are able to "bounce back" from traumatic life experiences. They still experience distress. However, they have the skill necessary to manage it effectively without developing long-term difficulties.

Resiliency is not a trait that people either have or do not have. It involves thoughts and actions that can be learned and developed by anyone. Relationships that create love and trust, provide role models and offer encouragement and reassurance help bolster a person's resilience.

The form of this Workbook is especially designed to support and guide you through a program that can lead to radical and lasting changes in our life and well-being. It is rare for such changes to come about just by reading about how we get entangled in emotional turmoil and what we can do to free ourselves. Rather, profound and lasting change usually involves taking some kind of "action" what, in this Workbook, we call "practice'. In this Workbook, the inner-healing work, processed one day at a time, that 99% of learning in TRIC goes on. Inner transformation depends on a continuing back-and-forth dance between understanding, practice, and reflection. The new insights and skills that merge are embodied deep in our souls—that is why they can have such widespread and enduring effects.

Dr. Sandy D. Murphy

In this *Session [I], What You DID and Didn't SAY*, you will learn that of all the knowledge and skills you have, those concerning communication will prove the most important and the most useful. The lack of communication has caused so many to become angry, confused, rejected, or become withdrawn from a relationship and/or marriage. Believe it or not, whatever form one communicates to another, it plays a significant part; [perhaps the most significant part] in all your relationships---from making friends and lifelong partners, to resolving inevitable conflicts, to networking for professional advantage, to working on a team solving problems, to informing and persuading large groups. Needless to say, but I will anyway, your communication knowledge and skills will always prove of value in all your interactions with other people, whether you're speaking or listening.

This *Session [I]* Workbook Series will **cover four** of *eight key communication components* crucial to this dance of spiritual *transformation: Relationship Development, Relationship Maintenance, Relationship Deterioration, Relationship Repair, Types of Friendships, Types of Lovers, Types of Primary Relationships, and Relationships Rules.* This study will also provide structure, a chance for reflection, and a source of light for inner-healing insight.

The **STRUCTURE** means: You will have a practical study lesson that will encourage, and strengthen you day by day along the journey of change. The study Building Skills, Reflections, Study Summary, Key Terms, and Thinking Critically post-study reviews will be featured in these series.

The **REFLECTIONS** is built in to the study focus of the Workbook. These positive communication lessons will give you the chance to pause, to stand back, and to see more clearly what is going on in your mind and body; as well as in the world around you. *From such reflections prophetic insights arise.*

The Workbook will support the development of **INSIGHT** by offering after each lesson a skills practice or exercise, and/or a participant's personal assessment to discover any inner-healing needs during or after each lesson.

<u>**ASSESS YOUR TRUST ATTITUDE:**</u> Please take a minute to complete the two page Trust SELF-Assessment Worksheet enclosed in back of this Workbook. This Assessment is designed to help us realize that oftentimes we assume the other person is at fault in a damaged trust relationship. However, by completing this Assessment, it will cause us to *"spiritually" look inside* to help us see if there's something we should own and/or change. This Assessment Tool is also great for Group Inner-healing Topical Discussions.

How CREDIABLE Are YOU?

As I prepared for this Session, I was led to review one of my favorite books, The Speed of Trust by Stephen Convey. After my quick review, I was spiritually moved to share some concepts of his four cores of credibility. Throughout this Session, you will see various segments from his principles of credibility.

The Self-Trust and Others Trust Assessment you completed earlier was only a short overview for you to closely look at your and others emotional state for inner-healing and to measure relationships "conditions" for spiritual development. As you read and process this Session, I encourage you to engage fully and truthfully in all the lessons. Please allow your heart to be purged to uproot the secret and painful matters that often cause us to become disloyal and reciprocate deceptive relationships.

Dr. Sandy D. Murphy

There was great revelation imparted after I read Mr. Covey's message regarding being credible to yourself and others from his first of four waves of Trust. He wrote that his first Wave of Trust should always be Self-Trust because self-trust is all about credibility. It's about developing the integrity, intent, capabilities, and results that make you believable, both to yourself and to others. And it all boils down to two simple questions: [1] *Do I trust myself?* [2] *Am I someone others can trust?*

One of the study modules that are required for our Clergy and Counselor Training is about Loyalty. It goes without saying that when clergy or anyone for that matter can't be trusted to even spend time with God or pray for themselves concerning issues that so easily best them, then why would we trust them to do anything larger; *like counsel or intercede for someone else!*

Mr. Covey stated that with regard to having trust in self, it often begins with the *"little"* things. Research shows that many of us don't follow through on the goals we set or don't keep the promises and commitments we make to ourselves.

So, Dr. Murphy, what happens when we do this time after time? What's the net result of repeated failure to make and keep commitments to ourselves? Every time we choose to disregard personal commitments, it simply chips away at our self-confidence. Not only do we lose trust in our own ability to make and keep commitments, we fail to project the personal strength of character that inspires trust.

Mr. Convey stated that we may try to borrow strength from "position or association". But...it's not real. It's not ours and people know it!
And whether we realize it or not, that impacts the

bottom line. As we explore our first of eight key communication components of Relationships, it is my prayer that you will understand that the lack of self-trust also undermines our ability to trust others. However, the good that can come from all of this is that every time we do make and keep a commitment to ourselves or set and achieve a meaningful goal, we become more credible. The more we do it, the more confidence we have that *we can* do it, and that *we will* do it. *The more we trust ourselves.*

WHAT IS TRUST?

Simply defined, trust means confidence and the opposite of trust is distrust/suspicion. When we trust people, we have confidence in them; in their integrity and in their abilities. But, when we distrust people, we are suspicious of them; of their integrity, their agenda, their capabilities or their track record of commitments. It's that simple. We all have had experiences that validate the difference between relationships that are built on trust and those that are not. These experiences clearly tell us the difference is not small; *it is traumatic.*

 *Ponderous Power Points*

You can have all the facts and figures, all the supporting evidence, all the endorsement that you want, but if you don't command trust, you won't get anywhere.
        ~Naill Fitzgerald, Former Chairman, Unilever.

[1]. RELATIONSHIP DEVELOPMENT

And the second is like, namely this, You shall love your neighbor as yourself. There is no other commandment greater than these. ~Mark 12:11

Most of our lives are focused on relationships; friendships, romantic relationships, and family relationships. These relationships occupy a great part of our daily lives, thoughts, and experiences. Interpersonal relationships come in various forms. Although the romantic relationship perhaps comes to mind most quickly, interpersonal relationships exist between friends, between mentors, and between work teams colleagues, to mention a few example. You establish your interpersonal relationships in stages. You don't become intimate with friends or with someone immediately upon meeting them. You should grow into an intimate relationship gradually, through a series of steps; from the initial contact, through intimacy, and perhaps on to dissolution. And the same is probably true with most other relationships as well.

Relationships are "spiritually living" things; they are forever changing sometimes for the good and sometimes not so good. There is probably nothing as important to most people as contact with others. This process is so important that when it's absent for a prolonged periods, depression sets in, self-doubt surfaces, and people find it difficult to conduct even the basics of daily living.

Relationship Development includes the initial contact stage as well as the increasing involvement and intimacy. People pursue a relationship for unique reasons; and there are also some general reasons for developing relationships: to lessen loneliness, to secure stimulation, to acquire self-knowledge, and to maximize pleasures and minimize emotional pain.

Take a minute right now and think of a person with whom you have a *high trust* relationship, perhaps a boss, pastor, mentor, coworker, customer, spouse, parent, sibling, child, or friend.

[1]. In the space provided below, briefly describe this relationship. [include: what it's like?, How does it make you feel?, and how well you communicate?]

_____
_____
_____
_____
_____

Think about the development of your own relationships as you read and answer the following questions.

[2]. *How quickly can you get things done together?*

_____
_____
_____
_____
_____
_____
_____
_____
_____

[3]. *How much do you enjoy this relationship?*

_____
_____
_____
_____
_____
_____
_____
_____

Now, think of a person with whom you have a *low-trust* relationship. Again, this person could be anyone at work, home, or church.

[4]. *Briefly describe this relationship.*

[5]. *What is unique about this relationship?*

[6]. *How does this relationship make you feel?*

_____
_____
_____
_____
_____
_____

[7]. *Does it flow quickly and freely? [explain how].*

_____
_____
_____
_____
_____
_____

[8]. *Do you feel like you are constantly walking on egg shells and being misunderstood?*

_____
_____
_____
_____
_____
_____

[9] *When you work together on business/ministry projects or home chores, do you tend to get things done quickly?*

[10] *Does it take an extreme amount of time and energy to finally reach agreement and execution about serious matters?*

[11] *Do you find your relationship at times to be too tedious, cumbersome, and draining?*

[2]. TYPES OF FRIENDSHIPS

Each relationship, whether friendship, love, or a primary relationship, is unique. Yet there are general types that research has identified; and these categories offer unusual insight into interpersonal relationships.

Everyday people are facing betrayal in some kind of way due the impact of Betrayal Trauma rather it comes through a friend or lover.

[A]. Relationships Types

There are *three major types* of friendships; reciprocity, receptivity, and association. The *"friendship"* of *Reciprocity*, the ideal type, is characterized by loyalty, self-sacrifice, mutual affection, and generosity. This type is based on equality. Each individual shares equally in giving and receiving the benefits and rewards of the relationship.

People who struggle with Betrayal Trauma often experience a great impact on their belief system. Their emotional and physical responses to trauma stemming from, betrayal are more likely to persist if the trauma changes the way they think about themselves and the world around them. When they begin to focus on the traumatic event, it tends to alter their beliefs about many issues, including their self-image, a sense of safety, sense of power and control or trust and intimacy in their relationships. If a person develop unhealthy beliefs in any of these areas, they may develop significant difficulties in their life.

Even after betrayal, a belief in your own worth is key to a healthy self-image. Countless numbers of people have negative thoughts about themselves after experiencing betrayal. They often find themselves engaging in unhealthy self-blaming, labeling themselves stupid, weak, bad, or worthless. Painful and negative voices often echo self-blame:

[A]. *Self-image:*

Do you think your self-image has been affected by Betrayal Trauma? [ ] Yes [ ] No
For either answer, please explain why.

_____
_____
_____
_____
_____

[B]. *Safety:*

Feeling safe is critical to a person's sense of well-being. Betrayal Trauma can alter a person's sense of well-being, leading them to view the world as an unsafe place. They also may doubt their ability to protect themselves from future traumatic events.

Do you feel capable of protecting yourself from future traumatic events?
[ ] Yes [ ] No
For either answer, please explain why.

_____
_____
_____
_____
_____
_____
_____
_____

The friendship of *Receptivity* [in contrast], there is an imbalance in giving and receiving; one person is the primary giver and the other the primary receiver. This is a positive imbalance, however, because each person gains something from the relationship. The different needs of both the person who receives affection and the person who gives it are satisfied. This type of friendship may develop between a teacher and a student or between a doctor and a patient. In fact, a difference in status is essential for the friendship or receptivity to develop.

The Friendship of *Association*. This type is transitory; it might be described as a friendly relationship rather than a true friendship. Association friendships are the kind we often have with classmates, neighbors, or coworkers. There is no great loyalty, no great trust, no great giving or receiving. The association is cordial but not intense.

Your obligation is to consider how you will use your perception with a certain type of relationship. Perception checking for relationships is another way to reduce uncertainty and to make perceptions more accurate. The goal of relationship perception is not to prove that your initial perception is correct, but to explore further the thoughts and feelings of the other person. With this simple method, you can lessen your chances of misinterpreting another's feelings. In most basic form, perception checking consists of two steps.
1. Describe what you see or hear, recognizing that even descriptions are not really objective but are heavily influenced by who you are, your emotional state, and so on.
2. Avoid "mind reading"; that is avoid trying to read other people's thoughts and feelings merely by observing their behaviors.

Regardless of how many behaviors you observe and how carefully you examine them, you can only guess what is going on in someone's mind.

Your obligation is to reveal yourself. At some point in any close relationship an ethical issue arises as to your obligation to reveal information about yourself.

[3]. TYPES OF LOVERS

Like friends. Lovers come in different styles as well as styles.

What will you do? Are there things you do to become more aware of the different love styles and to become a more well-rounded lover? Source {From "A Relationship-Specific Version of the Love Attitudes Scale" by C. Hendrick and S. Hendrick(1990).

1. *Eros Love:* Seeks beauty and sensuality and focuses on physical attractiveness, sometimes to the exclusion of qualities we might consider more important and more lasting. The erotic lover has an idealized imagine of beauty that is unattainable in reality. The Erotic lover often feels unfulfilled.

2. *Ludic Love*: Seeks entertainment and excitement and sees love as fun, a game. This type of relationship tends to be loose and

unfaithful. This type does not take love serious, emotions are to be held in check lest they get out of hand and make trouble. This type retains a partner only so long as the partner is interesting and amusing. When the partner is no longer interesting enough, it's time to change.

3. *Storge Love:* It is peaceful and tranquil love. Like Ludic, storge lacks passion and intensity. Storge lovers set out not to find a lover, but to establish a companion-like relationship with someone they know and with whom they can share interests and activities. Storge love is a gradual process of unfolding thoughts and feelings and is sometimes difficult to separate from friendship.

4. *Pragma Love:* It is practical and traditional and seeks compatibility and relationship in which important needs and desires will be satisfied. The Pragma Lover is concerned with the social qualifications of a potential mate even more than with personal qualities, family and background are extremely important to the program lover, who relies not so much on feelings as on logic.

5. *Manic Love:* It is an obsessive love that needs to give and receive constant attention and affection. When this is not given or received, or when an expression of increased commitment is not returned, reactions such as depression,

jealousy and self-doubt are often such as depression and can lead to the extreme lows characteristic of the manic lover.

6. <u>*Agape Love:*</u> This is compassionate and selfless. The agape lover loves both the stranger on the road and the annoying neighbor. Jesus, Buddha, and Gandhi practiced and preached this unqualified spiritual love; a love that is offered without concern for personal reward or gain and without any expectation that the love will be returned or reciprocated.

<u>The Betrayal Trauma Intimacy Risk Assessment</u>
Consider your own view of relationship risk by responding to the following questions.

1. Based on the truths about betrayal and deception being something considered as a norm, is it dangerous to get really close to people?

_____
_____
_____
_____
_____
_____
_____
_____

2. Are you afraid to get really close to someone because you feel that you might get hurt again?

_____
_____
_____
_____
_____

3. Do you find it difficult to trust people who you have not learned their faith or lifestyle?

_____
_____
_____
_____
_____

4. Do you believe that the most important thing to consider in a relationship is whether you might get hurt from a past or present issue?

_____
_____
_____
_____
_____

People who answer yes to these and similar questions see intimacy as involving considerable risk, such people have fewer close friends, are less likely to have a romantic relationship, have less trust in others, have a low level of dating assertiveness, have lower self-esteem are more possessive and jealous in their love, and are generally less sociable and extroverted than those who see intimacy involving little risk. **And by the way, not surprisingly, comfort with risk taking has been found to be common to people who make midlife career changes. (Ingram, 1998).**

TEST YOURSELF
What kind of Lover are you?

Respond to each of the following statements with [T] for true (if you believe the statement to generally accurate representation) of your attitude about love) or an [F] for false (if you believe the statement does not adequately represent your attitudes about love).

1. ____My lover and I have the right physical "chemistry" between us.
2. ____I feel that my lover and I were meant for each other.
3. ____My lover and I really understand each other.
4. ____I believe that what my lover doesn't know about me won't hurt him/her.
5. ____My lover would get upset if he/she knew of some of the things I've done with other people.
6. ____When my lover gets too dependent on me, I want to back off a little.
7. ____I expect to always be friends with my lover.
8. ____Our love is really deep friendship, not a mysterious, mystical emotion.

Dr. Sandy D. Murphy

9.____Our love relationship is the most satisfying because it developed from a good friendship.

10.____In choosing my lover, I believed it was best to love someone with a similar background.

11.____An important factor in choosing partner is whether or not he/she would be a good parent.

12.____One consideration in choosing my lover was how he/she would be reflect on my career.

13.____Sometimes I get so excited about being in love with my lover that I can't sleep.

14.____When my lover doesn't pay attention to me I feel sick all over.

15.____I cannot relax if I suspect that my lover is with someone else.

16.____I would rather suffer myself than let my lover suffer.

17.____Whne my lover gets angry with me, I still love him/her fully and unconditionally.

18.____I would endure all things for the sake of my lover.

Score details: The scale from Hendrick and Hendrick (1990) is based on the work of Lee (1976), as is the above defined six types of love. This scale is designed to enable you to identify your own beliefs about love. The statements refer to the six types of love. Statements 1-3 are characteristic of the Eros Lover. If you answered TRUE to these statements, you have a strong Eros component to your love style. If you answered FALSE, you have a weak Eros component. Statements 4-6 refer to Ludic Love, 7-9 to Storge Love, 10-12 to Pragma Love, 13-15 to Manic Love, and 16-18 to Agape Love.

Ponderous Power Points

"The only relationship in this world that have ever been worthwhile and enduring is and will always be an intimate relationship with God."

~Dr. Sandy Murphy

[4]. PRIMARY RELATIONSHIP

Thou shalt not bow down thyself to them, nor serve them: for I the Lord thy God am a jealous God, visiting the iniquity of the fathers upon the children unto the third and fourth generation of them that hate me; Exodus 20:5

The word "primary" means: *The main, chief, key, prime, central, principal, foremost, first, first-line, most important, predominant, paramount; fundamental basic, essential, initial, the original.*

While primary relationships are very important to family life, we are facing some critical changes, especially in single parent households. There are millions of single-parent households in the United States; but another critically obvious example of the increasing numbers of people living together in an exclusive relationship who are not married. Even worse, there are families on the rise that are headed by gay male or lesbian couples who live together as domestic partners or, in some cases spouses. Sadly, many of these couples have children from previous heterosexual unions, through artificial insemination, or by adoption.

The communication principles that apply to the term *primary relationship* denotes the relationship between the two principle parties; the husband and wife, the lovers, or the domestic partners, for example, just as the term *"family"* now may denote a broader constellation that includes children, relatives, and assorted significant others.

A *primary relationship* is a relationship between two people that the partners see as their most important interpersonal relationship. In view of this definition, a research conducted by Fitzpatrick Noller, identified three basic types of interpersonal relationships: *traditional, independents, and separates.*

Genesis 2:22: "And the rib, which the LORD God had taken from man, made he a woman, and brought her unto the man."

Traditional Couples: This type share basic belief system and philosophy of life. They see themselves as a blending of two persons into a single couple rather than as two separate individuals. They are interdependent and believe that each individual's independence must be sacrificed for the good of the relationship. They believe in mutual sharing and do little separately. Now this type appear to meet God's plan for marriage according to Genesis 2:22.

Matthew 19:5, "And said, For this cause shall a man leave father and mother, and shall cleave to his wife: and they twain shall be one flesh?"

Independents: They stress their individuality. The relationship is important to them, but never more important than each person's individual identity. The communication between independents is responsive. They engage in conflict openly and without fear. Their disclosures are quite extensive and include high-risk and negative disclosures that are typically absent among traditionals.

I Corinthians 7:2 , "Nevertheless, to avoid fornication, let every man have his own wife, and let every woman have her own husband."

Separates: They live together but view their relationship more as a matter of convenience than a result of their mutual love or closeness. They seem to have little in desire to be together and, in fact, usually are together only at ritual occasions such as a mealtime or holiday get-to-gethers. It is very important to these separates that each has his or her own physical and psychological space. Separates share little; each seems to prefer to go his or her own way. Separates hold relatively traditional values and beliefs about sex roles; and each person tries to follow the behaviors normally assigned to each role. What best characterizes this type is that each person sees himself or herself as a separate individual and not as a part of a "we."

Well, after this study, I can clearly see and I pray that you can too, that the current state of the Body of Christ fits the characteristics of the *"Independents" and "Separates."* So I guess this is why there is an epidemic of spiritual bastards and prodigal sons and daughters; *[and many are leaders of their own ministries]* who are *running spiritually naked* [souls/ministries uncovered] desperately trying to find authentic love, leadership enrichment from Kingdom-minded fathers and spiritual food to grow from. But instead, they face spiritual incest, prophetic liars, manipulation, and witchcraft to the point they don't trust no one! These are clear symptoms that they are suffering from intense Betrayal Trauma to the point that they can't discern the counterfeit from the authentically God-sent. Lord, Please HELP US All!

Did you know…… School and learning is liken to a building that has four walls with tomorrow's Kingdom purpose awaiting inside to be birthed.
~ Dr. Sandy Murphy

I just took a lunch break from this segment and God knows I am so glad I did! As I pondered on how so many Believers have literally made Pastors, First Ladies, Spouses, Money, Sex, Fame, Public Positions, Titles, and even Pets their primary God; needless to say it literally made my stomach nauseous! *Lord, HELP Us ALL Today!* Anyway, as I meditated on the state of our Nations and how we as Believers have become both too COMFORTABLE and/or have COMPROMISED about the spiritual warfare against Gay Rights issues, I started looking for cookies to calm my nerves! I thank God that I found NONE! So, I must release my voice here! *Put your spiritual seat-belt on; get off Facebook, Stop Texting, get yourself some strong tea, and listen to what the spirit of the Lord quickened me about.* Ok, here we go.....So now the Gay rights Groups has

joined together, created a pushed hard enough to get their deceptive/perverted Law passed that will allow gay/transgender populations to have the right to use any public Restroom based on any gender "they say" they are! So where were the Saints while they were meeting about laws that continue to tremendously spiritually impact our children in schools and colleges today? *I can take a quick shot at where the Saints were.* Keepin` it REAL---they were planning, fruitless "in-house" money-making so-called Revivals; *and worst of all,* flesh-gratifying events like a 100 Women in Red or the Pastor's Anniversary celebration. Calm down, and please let's not speak dishonorable towards me before you finish reading here. I honor leadership, and I truly believe we should demonstrate our honor for them. BUT, I find it hard to understand and TRUST the actions of those who spend more time "praying and saying", rather than doing something more than "inside-service" needs. The type of evangelical ministry that is critically deficient today in most *physical-building churches*, it is evangelical and discipleship equipping accountability practical training.

We spend too much time in our beautiful church buildings and complain about what the Gay Rights Groups are doing, while the "Believers" are acting jealous of each other because they either don't like a particular leader who sincerely want to host at social-action meeting at their church, while the jealous leader refuse to partner because their desire is to flaunt their vain-glory church decorations. So this self-glorifying plan to block or spiritually imprison one another continues to breed deceit while the lost [unsaved] looks on. Lord, help ME! I am not trying to preach here! But, this is how Betrayal Trauma ripples and spills over to the sheep who won't even share their salvation testimony, and worse of all, refuse to evangelize because it is too beneath them. Why? *Simply because, so goeth the head, so goeth the body.* Lord, send us ALL our personal Angels to SHAKE us who are asleep at the warfare gates and/or are those who are comfortably at ease in Zion!

TRUST MYTHS vs. REALITY
GAUGING YOUR TRUST LEVEL

Below is a Trust Myths & Reality Chart that provides examples of some myths that often get in the way of understanding and responding effectively to trust issues; along with their contrasting realities.

Myth	Reality
Trust is soft	Trust is hard, real, and quantifiable. It measurably affects both speed and cost.
Trust is slow	Nothing is fast as the speed of trust.
Trust is built solely on integrity	Trust is a function of both character (which includes integrity) an competence
You either have trust or you don't	Trust can be both created and destroyed.
Once lost, trust cannot be restored	Though difficult, in most cases lost trust can be restored.
You can't teach trust	Trust can be effectively taught and learned, and it can become leverage-able, strategic advantage.
Trusting people is too risky	Not trusting people is a greater risk.
Trust is established one person at a time	Establishing trust with the one establishes trust with the many.

Dr. Sandy D. Murphy

After reviewing this Chart, I hope that you can tell by now that Trust is HARD, it's REAL, and while recovering from Betrayal Trauma, it may take time to both establish and extend trust, but it can be done with the help of the Lord through forgiveness and the fruit of longsuffering. In order to reciprocate forgiveness and recover from betrayal, we MUST forgive. *Ephesians 4:32 - And be ye kind one to another, tenderhearted, forgiving one another, even as God for Christ's sake hath forgiven you.* The spirits of manipulation and control has been given willful access to both families, the Believers, and worst of faith leadership.

In my companion-Book for this Session entitled, *Why I Can't Trust You,* I mentioned how the spirit of Jezebel has worked boldly and overtime to control the church leadership; AND how it has switched faces with the spirit of Absalom to try and manipulate and deceive the Body of Christ through distrust and resentment of authority. The spirit of Absalom is rooted in independence and self-dependence; especially as it pertains to honest communication, problem solving, or sharing honest feelings, needs, special desires etc.

Just as Absalom deceived David and conspired to have him killed by close friend Ahithopel, this spirit is also rooted in hidden contempt, hidden hatred, and hidden revenge of any authority figure and those under authority. In times like these when the enemy is using the very elect, we must be prayerful to be able to see in the spiritual realm how the hidden agendas, deceptive strategies, and hidden religious alliances are taking root in the hearts and minds of leadership. As we face the spiritual warfare from the Absalom spirit who often sow seeds of rebellion to hurting sheep, causing them to believe that most church leadership is incompetent, not to be trusted, and that they have been gifted with leadership skills to lead people the "right way", we must remind them to take heed to Ephesians 6:5 that tells us: "Servants, be obedient to them that are your masters according to the flesh, with fear and trembling, in singleness of your heart, as unto Christ."

The disrespect of authority and self-promotion that the Absalom spirit often operates under-cover, and it will often manifest false humility, manipulation, disloyalty, religious hypocrisy, spiritual hype, and subtle emotional seduction. I consider the Absalom spirit as a hater and a faker because they work overtime to spiritually deceive those who have trust in righteous leadership. From my experience I have come to understand that they often manifest their betrayal through four key behaviors.

1. *Comparing:* They often compare their likeness or differences in leadership gifts. They put one gift, issue, or person by the side of another for the sake of comparison. **2.** *Compete*: They tend to contend or struggle in a battle or fight (spiritual and physical). They strive in dispute or debate. This means that they will strive (exert energy) or extreme effort to win or conquer an issue by any means necessary to win. This is a dangerous person! **3.** *Complain*: They will express feelings of dissatisfaction, resentment or emotional pain to make a formal accusation, or bring a charge against a person or an issue raised by authority. They will grumble, gripe, kick against, whine, or lie about an issue to get their way.

4. *Cunning:* They are skilled in deception, spiritually manipulative, shrewd, crafty, skillfully underhanded in performances, and controlling with the ability to restrain or influence direct authority. The bottom line is that they are rebellious and are operating in spiritual witchcraft!

As we have explored the issues that surround deceit, it has been proven that sin draws much strength from the fact that it dwells in the heart (which is ultimately deceitful and incomprehensible) and is pure enmity in all of the soul to all of God (Jer. 17:9). *In II Timothy 19*, Paul describes this kind of behavior as: "trucebreakers" who make no *conscience of the engagements they have laid themselves under. The times are truly perilous when men are false accusers one of another, diaboloi—devils one to another, having no regard to the good name of others, or to the religious obligations of an oath, but thinking themselves at liberty to say and do what they please.*

When men have no government of themselves and their own appetites, for they are incontinent; not of their own passions, for they are fierce; when they have no rule over their own spirits, and therefore are like a city that is broken down, and has no walls; they are soon fired, upon the least provocation. When that which is good and ought to be honored is generally despised and looked upon with contempt. It is the pride of persecutors that they look with contempt upon good people, though they are more excellent than their neighbors. When men are generally treacherous, willful, and haughty, the times are perilous when men are traitors, heady, and high-minded.

Our Savior has foretold that the brother shall betray the brother to death and the father the child (Matt, 10: 21). And those are the worst sort of traitors: those who delivered up their Bibles to persecutors were called traitors, for they betrayed the trust committed to them. When men are petulant and puffed up, behaving scornfully to all about them, and when his temper generally prevails, again, then the times are perilous. When men are generally lovers of pleasure more than lovers of God, and when there are more epicures than true Christians, then the times are bad indeed. God is to be loved above all. That is a carnal mind, and is full of enmity against him, which prefers anything before him, especially such a sordid thing as carnal pleasure is. When, notwithstanding all this, they have the form of godliness, are called by the Christian name, baptized into the Christian faith, and make a show religion; but, how plausible so-ever their form of godliness is, they deny the power of it. When they take upon them the form which should and would bring along with it the power thereof, they will put asunder what God hath joined together: they will assume the form of godliness, to take away their reproach; but they will not submit to the power of it, to take away their sin. Men may be very bad and wicked under a profession of religion; they may be lovers of themselves, and yet have a form of godliness. A form of godliness is a very different thing from the power of it; men may have the one and be wholly destitute of the other; yea, they deny it, at least practically in their lives.

From such good Christians must withdraw themselves. Paul warns Timothy to take heed of certain seducers, not only that he might not be drawn away by them himself, but that he might arm those who were under his charge against their seduction. He shows how industrious they were to make proselytes, they applied themselves to particular persons, visited them in their houses, not daring to appear openly; for those that do evil hate the light. (John 3:20). They were not forced into houses, as good Christians often were by persecution; but they of choice crept into houses to insinuate themselves into the affections and good opinion of people, and so to draw them over to their party. And see what sort of people those were that they gained, and made proselytes of; they were such as were weak, silly women; and such as were wicked, laden with sins, and led away with divers lusts. A foolish head and a filthy heart make persons, especially women, an easy prey to seducers. Paul also shows how far they were from coming to the knowledge of the truth, though they pretended to be ever learning. In one sense we must all be ever learning, that is, growing in knowledge, following on to know the Lord, pressing forward; but these were sceptics, giddy and unstable, who were forward to imbibe every new notion, under pretense of advancement in knowledge, but never came to a right understanding of the truth as it is in Jesus.

Paul also emphasizes the urgency to stop such behavior while, comparing them to the Egyptian magicians who withstood Moses, named, Jannes and Jambres. When Moses came with a divine command to fetch Israel out of Egypt, these magicians opposed him. Thus those heretics resisted the truth and like them were men of corrupt minds, men who had their understandings perverted, biased and prejudiced against the truth, and reprobate concerning the faith, or very far from being true Christians; but they shall proceed no further, or not much further. Seducers seek for corners, and love obscurity; for they are afraid to appear in public, and therefore creep into houses.

Further, they attack those who are the least able to defend themselves, silly and wicked women. Seducers in all ages are much alike. Their characters are the same-namely, Men of corrupt minds, and their conduct is much the same — they resist the truth, as Jannes and Jambres withstood Moses; and they will be alike in their disappointment. Those who resist the truth are guilty of folly, yea, of egregious folly; for great is the truth, and shall prevail. Though the spirit of error may be let loose for a time, God has it in a chain. Satan can deceive the nations and the churches no further and no longer than God will permit him: Their folly shall be manifested, and it shall appear that they are imposters, and every man shall abandon them." (Matthew Henry's Commentary on the Whole Bible)

On numerous occasions throughout the Gospels, Jesus goes to great lengths to clarify the nature of our Heavenly Father's relationship with us which is one of intimate fellowship, nurturing, care, and fatherly affection. All characteristics that warrant our complete t is found in Jesus' own words in Matthew 7:9-11. All across America families of all races and social economic status is under attack today. Every day spirits of anger, unforgiveness, control, and even murder has taken over the minds of hurting people. According to the 2002 Statistics of the U.S. Census Bureau one in two marriages in the United States will end in divorce. To further refine the raw data the report indicated that the: Average length of firs time marriages that end in divorce is 11 years, Percentage of college educated women who will divorce is 40%, and the Percentage of divorces occurring in the key child bearing years (2539) is 60%. In spite of the disheartening statistics, almost three quarters of adult Americans believe that marriage is a lifelong commitment that should not be ended except under extreme circumstances. (Excluding California, Colorado, Indiana, and Louisiana) Sadly to mention, we don't have the statistics for divorce rate among Christians; though I'm sure the numbers are regretfully high. Why? Pride keeps us silent due to the tormenting shame that the Body of Christ often inflict and the rejection towards those who refuse to stay in a physically and/or verbally abusive marriage!   Author Cindy

Hide reports in her book, 7 Steps to Divorcing Wisely, "One national survey of attorneys who specialize in marital law cited "a lack of commitment to the marriage" as the number one reason for divorce." Keeping it real, both men and women who suddenly find themselves in separation or divorce court did not happen from one big fight. The breach of trust is the ultimate reason!

People have *four basic needs* that must be met to maintain a healthy relationship. *These needs are as follows:* 1. *Acceptance:* This is the knowing that you are loved and needed by others. 2. *Identity:* This is realizing that you are individually significant and special. Identity also depicts who you are, where and who you came from (your bloodline, generation/family tree), what you own, if you are rich are poor, healthy, have a fruitful womb or a barren womb, bitter or unforgiving heart, healthy marriage or divorce, fornicating, or criminal bloodline etc. 3. *Security:* Believing that you are well protected and provided for. This also means that you are committed to protect and provide for those you love and vise verse.

4. *Purpose:* It is knowing that you have a reason for living and always seek to discover God's plan for your life. But, the some of the common reasons people get divorced are: poor communication,

financial problems, infidelity, drug addiction, physical, sexual or emotional abuse, religious beliefs, the lack of parental responsibility, and conflict resolution skills. So why is the family a frequent target for the enemy? The answer is simply because "family" is important to God. Nothing on this earth regarding you, apart from your salvation and obedience to the will for God, is as important to God as you family ties. A divorce in our nation occurs every twenty-seven seconds. Every year in the USA over 10 million women are battered by their husbands or an intimate partner. An estimated 3 million children witness family violence every year and children who grow up in abusive homes are more likely to drop out of school, abuse others, or become victims of violence as well. No matter what we are facing in our families today, we must never lose sight of the fact that satan is the source of all attacks against the family.

We must not only know spiritual warfare, but become experienced in spiritual warfare! We must not only know that to do in prayer, but we must actually intercede for our families. Spiritual warfare and obedience to the Word of God is our ultimate defense against assault from the enemy. Needless to, but I will anyway; the spiritual wellness state of the Body of Christ is in a critical state. Below is the

Barna Research reported: August 6, 2000. The report is entitled: America's "Christian" Health Chart.

The chart describes (4) Significant Vital Spiritual Wellness Signs about:
(1) Bible Truth (2) Professed Faith (3) Morality (4) Family) Regarding.......

- Biblical Truth - 78% of mainline Christians - 66% of "born-again" Christians do not believe in absolute truth. Only 9% of Christian youth and 4% of non-Christian youth embrace absolute truth.

- Professed Faith - 75% claim to be "Christian" in moral precept (a drop of 10% in one decade) - 45% claim to be "born-again" - 10% claim to be "evangelical."

- Morality - 75% of "Born again" Christians lie regularly and consciously - 18% of all abortions are among evangelicals - "No observable differences between moral behavior of professing Christians and rest of America." (Barna & Gallup) agree that their moral relation is now wrapped in a religious robe and declared righteous.

- Family - Divorce rate among "born-again" (new convert) Christians exceeds nation by 4% - Divorce rate among "Bible-believing" Saints exceeds nation by 50%........90% of all divorces among Christians occurred after they came to Christ. The deceptive spirit that is still working and must be destroyed among the Body of Christ that the researcher diagnosed is that….

- Jesus may be "Savior" <u>but SELF is king.</u>

And that a great number of American "Christians" do not worship the God of the Bible, but "a custom-made God, one made in their own SELFISH image".

The FOUR Selves
As in water face answereth to face, so the heart of man to man. Proverbs 27:1

As I prepare to close this Session, I realized that I dare not close before I share one of the most critical elements in communication; the SELF-Concept. The bible tells us in James Chapter 1: 23-25, *"For if any be a hearer of the word, and not a doer, he is like unto a man beholding his natural face in a glass: For he beholdeth himself, and goeth his way, and straightway forgetteth what manner of man he was. But whoso looketh into the perfect law of liberty, and continueth therein, he being not a forgetful hearer, but a doer of the work, this man shall be blessed in his deed."* So many silently suffer with Betrayal Trauma to the point that they often battle with being "on guard" all the time. They become irritable or suddenly angry. The memories of the traumatic experience cause nightmares or other images of betrayal suddenly "pop" into their heads at any given time.

Survivors who have faced emotional pain that traumatized them by a faith leader [or church member] often view faith leaders as

deceptive, manipulative, controlling, hypocritical, and/or they often see their world as filled with danger; so their minds and bodies are on constant alert, always ready to respond immediately to any possible attack. Learning who you are, how you perceive yourself and others greatly influence your communications and your responses to the communications of others. I hope to help you learn in this segment how *self-concept, self-awareness, self-esteem, self-disclosure, the Four Selves*, and how they all work in communicating offense or blatant betrayal.

Self-Concept: This is your image of who you are. It's how you perceive yourself: your feelings and thoughts about your strengths and weaknesses and your abilities and limitations. It develops from the image that others have of you and reveal to you; the comparisons you make between yourself and others; your cultural experiences in the realms of race, ethnicity, gender, and gender roles; and your evaluation of your own thoughts and behaviors.

Example: The looking-glass self [or mirror image], you would look at this image of yourself that others reveal to you through their behaviors and especially through the way they treat you and react to you. These are the people who are most important or significant in your life.

Self-Awareness: **It is the practical: the more you understand yourself, the more you'll be able to control your thoughts and behaviors.**

> **Take time to make a LIST in the space provided below of YOUR OWN interpretations and evaluations of specific qualities you have or hope to become better at. This will help you self-assess your strengths and weaknesses that may have been wounded or rejected by others.**

1.
2.
3.
4.
5.
6.
7.
8.
9.
10.
11.
12.

The FOUR Selves

	Known to Self	Not known to Self
Known To Others	**OPEN SELF** Information about yourself that you and others know	**BLIND SELF** Information about yourself that you don't know, but that others do know
Not Known To Others	**HIDDEN SELF** Information about yourself that you know, but others don't know	**UNKNOWN SELF** Information about yourself that neither you nor others know

Let's pretend that the above four Selves represent you. The OPEN SELF represents all the information, behaviors, feelings, desires, motivations, ideas, and so on that you know about yourself and that others also know. The BLIND SELF represents information about yourself that others know, but you don't. This may vary from relatively insignificant quirks, using the expressions "you know" rubbing your nose when you get angry, or having a peculiar body odor, to something as significant as defense mechanisms, fight strategies, or repressed experiences. Although we may be able to shrink our blind areas, we can never eliminate them. The UNKNOWN Self represents those parts of yourself about which neither you nor others know. This is the information that is buried in your unconscious or that has somehow escaped notice. You gain insight into the unknown self from a variety of different sources. The HIDDEN SELF contains all that you know about yourself and others. At extremes of this of this quadrant are over-disclosers.

Growing in Self-Esteem has to do with the way you feel about yourself; how much you like yourself, how valuable a person you think you are, how competent you think you are. These feelings reflect the value you place on yourself; they're a measure of self-esteem. Although self-esteem depends largely on achieving your goals, your culture seems to select the specific goals. Below are a few self-esteem suggestions to assist with increasing your self-esteem.
  a. Attack beliefs that are self-destructive
  b. Seek out people who will be nurturing
  c. Secure affirmation
  d. Work on projects that will prove successful.

Now that you have some considerations for your self-esteem, below are some Self-Affirmations to consider as well. Briefly complete the fragmented statements by sharing your feelings about your Self-Affirmations.

1. I'm a worthy person, though there's room for improvement in……

_____
_____
_____

2. I am generally responsible and can be depended upon for or when……

_____
_____
_____

3. I'm capable of loving and being loved because……

_____
_____
_____

4. I deserve good things to happen to me because……

_____
_____
_____

5. I can forgive myself for mistakes and misjudgments because…….

_____
_____
_____

6. I deserve to be treated with respect because…….

_____
_____
_____

Dr. Sandy D. Murphy

Making TRUST Personal

As you think about behaving in ways that build trust, keep in mind that every interaction with every person is a "moment of trust." The way you behave in that moment will either build or diminish trust. How you behave with your spouse or friendships is noticed by others. By behaving responding to or behaving in ways that build trust with one, you will build trust with many. *Below are a few questions for you to answer* in order to help you determine what your Trust account balance is like; and to give you the opportunity to look back, identify, the two or three behaviors that would make the greatest difference for you, and create an actionable plan for change. I encourage you to make this segment highly relevant and personal for your personal life.

1. Do you feel like you are struggling to communicate well with your spouse?

_____
_____
_____

2. Do you feel like you keep picking the same person over and over again to be in a relationship with only to find that they are unfaithful and it doesn't work out?

___

3. Are you finding it a challenge to build meaningful friendships after being betrayed?

___

4. Are you having difficulties with co-workers at your place of employment who plot to set traps for your work to appear inadequate?

___

5. Does your partner complain that they feel unable to connect with you?

___

6. Do you feel alone in a crowd at times, unable to figure out how to join in and be interconnected with those around you?

___

We all struggle with relationships in different ways. Learning how to be in a relationship with others is something that most of us get "on the job" training in. Relationships are both art and science and learning how to do them well is one of life's great tasks.

 *Ponderous Power Points*

You should not be satisfied with being a victim, nor with being a survivor. You should aim to be a conqueror. There is an extraordinary quality of spirit that leads one to aspire to conquering rather than surviving. I hope you discover that spirit in yourself." ~ By: Dr. Laura Schlessinger

HOW TRUST WORKS

Dynamics of Trust:

a. *Trust is earned over time.* **Seldom is trust bestowed. It is almost without exception, the results of real precedents, real actions.**

b. *Trust and general morality.* **Across all ages, human existence has produced general ideas of what is moral and what is immoral. While there are certainly times when "rules" and "laws" have to be modified to meet the demands of specific situations, the general rules of human conduct, respect, and decency that have been established are predominately helpful and have good outcomes in mind.**

c. *When trust is broken:* **I is almost unrealistic to think that there would not be times when trust will be broken. Some people are able to forgive, but they may never forget the betrayal because something tied to the breach in the trust relationship hangs back there in the recesses of our minds forever. I'm talking about those breeches in trust when we have not followed through, kept commitments adequately, or**

Dr. Sandy D. Murphy

performed at the level of expectation required. So, Dr. Murphy, how do we bounce back from the pain of betrayal? Well, the first step is repentance and second honesty.

d. *Trust processes:* In most of our interactions with other human beings in the modern world we live in, there is not direct contact. Instead, we made contact with others through the products and processes that we create or take part in delivering. Think for a few minutes about all that you do that does not bring you into direct contact with another person, but that has a real impact or influence on the life of another person.

e. *Avoiding "behind-the-scenes" politics:* When trust prevails, there is an atmosphere in which people, as adults, bring issues "to the top of the table" where they can be discussed, modified, refined, integrated until some sort of consensus, middle ground, or more conclusive decision can be made. If the atmosphere is right, all kinds of discussion and dissent can prevail until a decision is made; then, the group decision becomes the decision of the individuals in the group. When everything is "on the table," difference of opinion and belief can be vented, but trust can be preserved.

My TRUST Testimony: **While there are many faith-walks I can share, but I want to briefly share an experience I learned from trusting "too soon." Early into my ministry I had the opportunity to apply for a Grant for my ministry and wanted to share the details with the Board of Directors. Well, as all ministries who are seeking to build Kingdom and do the right thing by explaining the Grant and the funding opportunities we would have to begin our Gang Prevention outreach. Once the Board realized I was going to have a great chance to receive the Grant, the same night of our meeting, three of the Executive Board Members conspired to move me out of my own ministry. *Yes... my Judas slipped in on the Grant.* I became restless and fearful about what they not only said to me, but their behavior was blatantly evil! When they saw that I was regretful for choosing them to be a Board Member, the Chairman and the Secretary left the ministry, took our legal documents with them, and refused to return them. I guess you are wondering, why would they do that? It was simply GREED! They wanted to control the ministry funding based on the "possibility," that we would get the Grant. Well, that act of deception from them helped me to realize that I chose those two Judas mindsets based on their** leadership titles, rather than seeking God about their heart conditions to humbly serve this ministry. It took me several months to forgive them for their betrayal. Without even thinking of them, the Betrayal Trauma would revisit me at different occasions when doing ministry business, especially when issues might appear to be happening like I experienced with them. *[end of testimony]*

In almost any discussion of trust, keeping commitments comes up as the number one influencing behavior. Even though to "keep commitments" is one of those behaviors that seem obvious and is just plain common sense, as the expression goes, *"Common sense is not always common practice."* And the impact on trust is devastating.

As I learned that day from the betrayal of those Board Members, [and have learned on almost every level of leadership from that day on]. Trust is one of the most powerful forms of motivation and inspiration. Let's face it, people want to be trusted. They respond to trust. They thrive on trust. Whatever the situation, we need to get good at establishing, extending, and restoring trust; not as a manipulative technique,

but as the most effective way of relating to and working with others, and the most effective way of getting results. In order to do that, we first need to understand how trust works. From this day forward, please consider asking yourself the following questions:
a. Who do you trust?
b. Why do you trust them?
c. Why do you trust a friend?
d. Why do you trust a workplace associate?
e. Why do you trust your boss?
f. Why do you trust your child?
g. Why do you trust your spouse?

Now, let's consider an even more provocative question. **WHO TRUSTS YOU?**
a. People at home?
b. A parent?
c. People at work?
d. Someone you just met?
e. Someone who has known you for a long time?
f. What is it in you that inspires the trust of others?

Most of us think about trust in terms of position, public opinion, or character, of being a good or sincere person or having ethics or integrity. And

Character is absolutely foundational and essential. But, as I explained in the message above, to think that trust is based on character only is a myth. Trust is a function of two key things: *character and competence.* Character includes your integrity, your motive, and your intent with people and criminal history. Competency includes your capabilities, your skills, your professional services results, and your successes track record. And both are very vital.

JOURNAL OF STRENGTH

"Fear thou not; for I am with thee; be not dismayed; for I am thy God: I will strengthen thee; yea I will help thee; I will uphold thee with The right hand of righteousness" Isaiah 41:10

Trust Recovery WORKBOOK

Working "OUT"
My Painful Past

Dr. Sandy D. Murphy

Working "OUT" My Painful Past

1. Do you find it difficult to trust anyone? [ ] Yes [ ] No
   If yes, Briefly explain why you have trouble trusting people. Include what age, gender, relationship, or title your distrust began with and about what?

   _____
   _____
   _____
   _____
   _____
   _____
   _____

2. Do you find it difficult in keeping a healthy relationship?
   [ ] Yes [ ] No
   If yes, What do you feel is causing your relationship(s) to fail?

   _____
   _____
   _____
   _____
   _____

3. Do you expect people to leave you? [ ] Yes [ ] No
   If yes, Why do you feel this way?

   _____
   _____
   _____
   _____
   _____

4. Is it hard for you to say NO to people when they ask you to do something that you know you do not want to do? [ ] Yes [ ] No
   If yes, Do you do this because you fear being rejected or are you afraid to say no for other reasons? Explain:

   _____
   _____
   _____
   _____
   _____

5. Is it easier to make friends and keep them, but you find it hard to work through issues with your lover or spouse? [ ] Yes [ ] No
   If yes, Explain why.

   _____
   _____
   _____
   _____

6. Do you often feel taken advantage of? [ ] Yes [ ] No
   If yes, Explain why.

   _____
   _____
   _____
   _____
   _____

7. Do you often feel that you find yourself changing relationships because the person may remind you of your betrayer?
   [ ] Yes [ ] No

If yes, What do you feel is the emotional trigger(s) that remind you of the betrayer when you are with this person?

_____
_____
_____
_____
_____

8. Do you find yourself often getting involved in relationships that are incompatible or abusive (emotionally or physically)?
   [ ] Yes [ ] No

If yes, What emotions do you feel may be causing you to choose these types of relationships?

_____
_____
_____
_____
_____

9. Do you feel absent (leave your body) when making love?
[ ] Yes [ ] No -If yes, What explain what happens to you.
_____
_____
_____
_____

10. Do you try to use sex to meet special needs that you want that aren't sexual? [ ] Yes [ ] No
If yes, Explain why you feel you need to do this.
_____
_____
_____
_____
_____
_____

11. Do you often find yourself trying to avoid sex or seeking to have sex when you really don't want it? [ ] Yes [ ] No
If yes, Explain what you are feeling when this happens.
_____
_____
_____
_____
_____

12. Are you involved in a relationship that is sexually abusive?
[ ] Yes [ ] No
If yes, Explain why you tolerate this relationship?
_____
_____
_____
_____

13. Do you feel you have to be perfect? [ ] Yes [ ] No
If yes, Why do you feel this way?
_____
_____
_____
_____
_____

14. Do you have a hard time nurturing yourself? [ ] Yes [ ] No
If yes, Why?

_____
_____
_____
_____
_____

15. Do you have trouble expressing your true feelings to others?
[ ] Yes [ ] No - If yes, Why?

_____
_____
_____
_____
_____

16. Do you frequently feel confused about simple issues?
[ ] Yes [ ] No - If yes, Why?

_____
_____
_____
_____
_____

17. Are you able to recognize your true feelings and tell the difference between denial and truth? [ ] Yes [ ] No
If yes, Explain how you are able to do this.

_____
_____
_____
_____
_____

IMPORTANT NOTE: *If you answered YES to just ONE of ANY of the previous questions, then you should seek professional counseling now.*

Factors That Promote Support & Recovery

- Offer a safe, comfortable, and non-judgmental environment
- Personal outreach, the development of a social network, the "therapeutic community" gift of being present, listening, and friendship to a validating environment to victims/survivors
- Demonstrate a spirit of hospitality, expressed by both clergy and congregants, this will serve as a welcoming beacon of hope
- Clergy need to know when and where to refer a person with emotional abuse issues, and also know how to support that person in the congregation.
- Counseling Staff or Congregant Care leaders need tools to help them incorporate spiritually into their places of inner-healing techniques.
- Offer an opportunity for self-disclosure, for victims/survivors to tell their stories to forge connections in a spirit of trust and acceptance.
- Foster recovery through prayer (personal and congregational, formal and informal), personal testimony, Bible study, fasting, scripture meditation and memory.
- Offer cultural diversity/sensitivity classes to understand sexual abuse and the various religious taboos that cause victims to stay in abusive environments or relationships.
- Develop age appropriate education and training programs for clergy, leaders, parents, or *special needs* congregants to understand the values, role of faith, and spirituality in healing.

- Offer ***Emotional Recovery*** support group sessions that will address emotional trauma from rejection, fear, shame, sexual identity issues, sexual abuse, domestic violence, etc. and on how to integrate natural healing (medicine practices) as deemed necessary.
- Reach beyond the church and grassroots organizations to build a bridge of hope for victims/survivors that will focus on mental health issues, including discrimination and stigma in housing, insurance issues, the criminal justice systems, and drug, alcohol, addictions.
- Allocate resources to undertake special programs that will influence social policy and bring about social justice for victims/survivors.
- Encourage collaboration and interaction among faith-communities, consumers, family members, advocates, healthcare providers, community organizations, and government agencies. Provide incentives to bring communities and churches together to implement recommendations.
- Compile a list of "best practices" models and resources and develop strategies to share lessons learned.

Closing Empowerment Points

Building *Resilience* from *Betrayal Trauma*

I am a survivor and I am *socially-active in thriving to advocate* against physical, emotional, mental, spiritual, or sexual abuse, incest, rape and the alike. Just like you, I was concerned about how the religious taboo of denial would affect my family. You are a SURVIVOR and a THRIVER. You are no longer a VICTIM! If you are ready to fight back and take action to counteract the negative images from your past, about how the victims/survivors are being portrayed in social networks, the uneducated church, faith relationships, and close friends.

BELOW are [9] Resilience Building Skills to strengthen resilience that you may find effective in your inner-healing journey.

1. ***Make connections:*** Accept help from those who care about you and will listen to you. Think about how your support networks can help you recover.

2. ***Avoid seeing crisis as insurmountable problems.*** You can't change the fact that highly stressful events happen, but you can change how you interpret and respond to these experiences. Focus on how you see your issue getting better in the future.

3. ***Begin to trust yourself by moving toward your goals:*** Develop some realist goals. Do something regularly; even if it seems like a small step; that enables you to move toward your goals. Instead of focusing on task that seem unattainable, ask yourself, *"What's one thing I know I can accomplish today that helps me move in the direction I want to go?"*

4. ***Accept that change is a part of life:*** Certain goals may no longer be attainable as a result of your recovery process. Realizing that inner-healing is a divine process that you can embrace one day at a time. Take time to journal some issues that you can change now that will not cause backlash during your recovery.
5. ***Take decisive actions:*** Act on opposing situations as much as you deem necessary. Take decisive action rather than detaching completely from frustrations, or stressful problems, and wishing that they would just go away. Try to focus on the situation, develop a healthy strategy and act on it. Journal at least one decisive action you can take as situations arise.
6. ***Look for opportunities for self-discovery:*** People often learn something about themselves and may find that they have grown in some respect as a result of their emotional struggle. Many people who have experienced Betrayal Trauma have recovered and are experiencing better relationships, a greater sense of strength and self-worth, a more developed spirituality and a heightened appreciation for life.
7. ***Maintain a hopeful and grateful outlook:*** An optimistic outlook and a grateful attitude enables you to expect that good things will happen in your life. Try visualizing what you want, and hope for, rather than worrying about what you fear could happen from your past hurtful experiences.
8. ***Nurture a positive view of yourself:*** Developing confidence in your ability to solve problems and trusting your instincts will help build greater resilience. As you learn to trust your instincts and your ability to solve problems, facing personal, ministry, or family challenges will be less stressful. Include in your journal the name of a specific problem that you recently solved and how you conquered it without becoming emotionally drained or stressed about it.
9. ***Take Good Care of Yourself:*** Please pay attention to your own emotional and physical needs. Engage in activities that you enjoy find relaxing. Exercise regularly. Taking care of yourself helps to keep your mind and body primed with situations that require resilience. Take time to journal some things that you do that demonstrates taking good care of yourself.

Regardless to what you may hear from family, friends or even the church, trust your own sense of who you are and what your experience have been. The greatest part of your healing process will be about learning to trust yourself, your feelings, and your reality. Only you and God know the truth about what really happened to you. Continue to value your own knowing about what happened, even if that changes as you discover more from your painful past.

Stay Educated: Even though your personal experience is valid in itself, it can help to have more information available from other educational resources; such as: books or tapes on healing from incest, molestation, rape, shame, anger, fear, unforgiveness, posttraumatic stress etc. It is ok if you don't do anything to reach out right away. Many survivors see the need to do something, but they're still in the vulnerable stages of their own healing, they're not in a position to respond themselves. Remember, your own inner-healing is your first responsibility. As you grow stronger, you can begin to share your strength with others to help them begin to break the silence, but it's critical that you take care of yourself first!

I can admit that in this perilous day in time we have made some strides in recognizing and dealing with Emotional Trauma. However, we still have much more to do to impact education to survivors and families through the greatest venue that has been shut to these issues, and that is the CHURCH! The church must begin to realize that victims of all types from PTSD, Depression, incest, domestic violence, rape, and even pedophiles are sitting on the pews and even serving in leadership positions; yet no one will be bold enough to speak up and say........."*We're taking a stand and fighting for our children and families against abuse of any kind!*"

I along with millions of advocates and survivors have challenged the church and others in government power who can help bring greater exposure to the ever-increasing horrific epidemic of mental, emotional abuse, and violence; but our cry for global change seems to only get an "annual" *occasional ear*. The current backlash against survivors of childhood sexual abuse is a destructive, undermining force, and the use of that force has been spiritually intentional as it relates to spiritual incest. This is a family and church matter! The bible tells us......."*And a man's foes shall be they of his own household.*"(Matthew 10:36). Therefore, we must be vigilant in the power of God's might.

"The Kingdom suffereth violence, and the violent must take it by force! (Personal emphasis/fragmented scripture) Matt. 11:12. God knows we are truly at a crossroad. As a faith society we must continue to fight for the souls of every child and family for the healing of every survivor, or we can give in to our collective denial and once again bury the TRUTH! It is critical that we reaffirm our commitment to children, to adults who have been abused, and to stopping the abuse that is still going on.

Children continue to be abused in horrific large numbers, adult survivors continue to suffer, and families struggle to come to terms with these violations. We have progressed from silence about abuse to awareness, yet there must be *"hands on work"* and a *voice of change* to be heard *from the pulpit* that must be done now! The church needs to be active in the change process against these spiritual epidemics. We as faith-leaders need to find space in our beautiful churches and offices, and establish an environment where survivors of Emotional Trauma, dating, marriage/family matters, and/or child sexual abuse can come and be believed and where the protection of the victim or survivor's inner-healing is a priority.

We need to create a climate that encourages honesty rather that defensiveness, where people who have been abused can acknowledge their behavior and be accountable, rather than cover up the truth for peace sake and further reinforce their denial. We need programs in the church and faith-based organizations in which offenders can get help in stopping their abuse as well as help in their own healing. This is critical. Educating the public, helping survivors heal, and prosecuting abusers are all very necessary, but we must also stop people from abusing.

"The essence of this tragedy is that it can never be fully communicated........

And yet, we are duty-bound to try. Not to do so would mean to forget. To forget would mean to kill the victims a second time......

Memory is not only a victory over time, it is also a triumph over injustice" ~by, Elie Wiesel

Dr. Sandy D. Murphy

It is a proven fact that we will become a prisoner of what we believe even if it's a lie! When we believe a lie, it becomes truth to you even though it is not actually truth at all. Do a self-test to see if you trust yourself more than God. Never trust yourself! Always lean on the Word of God because what we believe is right in our eyes is more than likely wrong through the eyes of God! (cf. Prov. 14:12). The heart is deceitful above all things, and it is exceedingly perverse and corrupt and severely, mortally sick! Who can know it (perceive, understand, be acquainted with his own heart and mind).
Read: Jer. 17:5-10

Father, In Jesus Name, I thank you that the reader or whoever this book is given to, it has made an impact in their life today; and that they have made a new step toward healing in their lives. I pray that by the power and authority of the Blood and Cross of Jesus Christ that every door is shut from the dark and evil thoughts in your mind. I speak love and peace to your conscience, and broken heart; and I release healing and freedom to your fragmented soul. In Jesus Name, Be Whole! Amen.

Every day or whenever you find yourself thinking of your painful past, recite these words below to yourself.

In Jesus Name, According to Cols 2:10 ……."I am *loved*, I am *whole*, and I am *complete* in Him who is the head of all principality and power!" *In Jesus' Name, Amen*

Corporate Prayer

Father, In the Name of Jesus I come today to repent for all the sins and iniquities that so easily beset me. I am making a decision today to break all unrighteous authority, manipulation, or control exercised over me. I renounce all unrighteous covenants and I loose myself from all unrighteous or controlling relationships. I offer my body as a living sacrifice to you Lord and I choose to walk in holiness. Through the power of the Blood and love of Jesus, I declare that the spirit of deception is destroyed and I loose the Spirit of Truth over my mind to lead me into all truth according to your Word and purpose for my life. I declare by the Blood of Jesus that I am free and the Spirit of Truth leads me in the path of righteousness and He is always with me. In Jesus' Name! Amen

Have You Decided To Trust Jesus As Your Personal Savior?

Do you desire a personal relationship with the One who created you and loves you no matter what? If so, tell Him in your own words or use this simple prayer below:

Heavenly Father,
I acknowledge that I am a sinner in need of Your forgiveness. I believe that Jesus fully paid the penalty for all my sin by dying at Calvary, and that He rose from the dead. Thank You for Your grace

Dr. Sandy D. Murphy

and mercy to save me though I am undeserving. I surrender my heart to You. Please show me how to start living a righteous life to glorify You.
In Jesus Name, Amen.

If you prayed this prayer of salvation, I want to personally welcome you to the Body of Christ. I would love to assist you in any way possible to help you take your next step in your walk with God. One of the greatest ways to keep yourself connected in your new faith-walk is to study the Word of God, and share your Testimony about how God saved you to others.

I would love to hear you share your testimony with me! Please email or call me at: eladysons@gmailcom OR (281) 372-0037.

May God richly bless you as you embrace your faith-journey.

SUGGESTED BOOKS & STUDY REFERENCES

Why I Can't Trust You, Dr. Sandy Murphy
King James Version Bible
The New Strongs Expanded Bible Dictionary of Words
American Standard Bible
Vine's Expository Dictionary of New Testament Words, © 1985
New Unger's Bible Dictionary
Webster's New World Dictionary
New King James Version Bible
Human Communications, Joseph DeVito
Man's Question, God's Answer
Trauma in Life, The Change Company
The Soul Care Bible
Man's Question, God's Answer
Life Principals Bible
The Trust Advisor, Dr. David Miaster
Spirit for Greatness, Dr. C. Stephen Byrum
J. Hampton Keathley III – ©2004-Bible Study
The Message Bible
The Speed of Trust, Stephen Covey
Seven Steps To Divorcing Wisely
Protecting Your Family, Dr. Charles Stanley
Kairos Human Analytics

WHERE TO FIND HELP AND INFORMATION

If you would like individual counseling, have questions, you are a parent and need help for yourself, or want to report a case of abuse, please call Now!

Emergency Hotlines:

Building Better Families-Fair Care Center, Inc. We have been organized since 1990 as a non-profit, 501c3 tax-exempt organization. We offer FREE Behavior Wellness Assessments, counseling service scholarships are available for clients who meet the requirements, and affordable sliding scale service fees. We offer faith-based and secular counseling for Individual, Family, Groups, Relationships or Marriages. For your FREE confidential personal consultation call now!

CALL 24 HOURS A DAY: (832) 303-2451 **OR** (281) 372-0037
Email: betterfamily3@gmail.com
Website: www.buildbetterfamilies.webs.com

The services below offers emergency help, referral to area services, information about reporting and more, look in front of the phone book under "Community Service Numbers" or call the National Child Abuse Hotline. 1-800-422-4453

Family Services Agencies
These listed below may offer childcare, emergency shelter, and other family support services. Look in your yellow pages under "Family Services" and "Social Services" for providers in your area.

Child Protective Services
This is the state agency that handles child abuse reports, and protects children. Call a hotline, or look in the white pages under your state's government listings. http://www.dir.state.tx.us

National Council on Child Abuse and Family Violence
1-800-222-2000

COPYRIGHTS & SUPPORT RESOURCES
Copyrights

- Texas Intermediate Child Abuse Instructor Guide, 2001 Edition
- Center For Disease Control
- U.S. Department of Health & Human Services- Building Bridges, Mental Health Consumers and Members of Faith-based and Community Organizations
- Subconscious Communications for Interview & Interrogations, S.A. Rhoades, Ph.D. 1981/2004
- The Courage To Heal, Ellen Bass and Laura Davis
- The National Child Protective Authority, No. 330 Thalawothugoda Rd. Madlwela
- Elie Wiesel, "For the Dead and the Living, We Must Bear Witness", Bostonia, 2 (Summer 1993) pg. 15.
- Human Communications, Joseph DeVito
- The Speed of Trust, Stephen Covey
- Seven Steps To Divorcing Wisely
- Kairos Human Analytics
- Trauma in Life, The Change Company
- The Trust Advisor, Dr. David Miaster
- Spirit for Greatness, Dr. C. Stephen Byrum

Resources

- Specialized Training Services: www.specilaizedtrainingservice.com, 1-800-848-1226
- Office of Violence Against Women: www.ojp.usdoj.gov/vaw0
- National Domestic Violence Hotline: 1-800-799-7233, www.ansers.com/topics/social-networking-site
- www.projectsafeneighborhood.com
- http://www.ncvc.org
- www.taasa.org
- http://www,vaw.umn.edu/library/
- Women's Advocacy Project, www.women-law.org, 1-800-374-4673
- National Clearinghouse on Child Abuse & Neglect: www.calib.com/nccanch - 1-800-553-4539
- Posttraumatic Stress Disorder Alliance, www.ptsdalliance.org 1-877-507-PSTD
- Survivors of Incest Anonymous, Inc. – www.siawso.org, 410-893-3322

Dr. Sandy D. Murphy

Dr. Apostle Sandy D. Murphy
Service/Professional Vitae
Author, Teacher, Advocate, Counselor

P.O. Box 15211- Humble, Texas 77347
(281) 372-0037 ~(Personal) Email: eladysons@gmail.com
www.elected.webs.com - www.buildbetterfamilies.webs.com

Education
PhD Counseling In Education – G. M.O. Theological Institute
Certified Faith-based Marriage & Family Therapy- Therapon Institute
Certified Belief Therapist- Therapon Institute
Certified Texas Workforce Commission Exempt Proprietary School Provider
Certified Texas State Board CEU Provider for Social Work & Counseling
Certified Faith-based TCADA Drug/Alcohol Prevention Counseling Provider
Certified Family Wellness Instructor
Certified P.A.P.A. Instructor
Certified Strengthening Families Instructor
Certified Anger Management/Domestic Violence Facilitator

Service & Secular Work Experience
On September 6, 1974, her then husband shot her between the eyes at close range with a twelve-gauge shotgun. Even though the entire right side of her face was almost blown completely away, she miraculously survived. Dr. Murphy is a survivor of incest, rape, and domestic violence. Today over 43 years later, Sandy Murphy is a living testimony of God's Miracles, Mercy & Grace to the lost and hurting, especially battered and abused, women, men, and children. Sandy has a Doctorate in Counseling Education/Marriage & Family Therapy for broken families, individuals, or ex-offenders. She serves in the chosen and anointed call as an Apostle, and moves by the Holy Spirit in the ministry of "inner-healing and deliverance" for spiritually wounded and lost souls. She is the Overseer/Servant of WHOLE-Family Healing & Deliverance Center, WHOLE-Family Lifelines Ministry [Cyber Church], Host & Executive Producer of The Dr. Keepin` It REAL TV Show, BlogTalk Radio Show, WHOLE-Woman Wednesday TV Show, Executive Producer of ASK Real MEN Monday TV Show, and Founder/Chancellor of Elect Lady Sons of Thunder School of Ministry & Mentoring Academy and WHOLE-Woman Books University; Sandy has been speaking professionally for over 37 years. By profession and through the gift of Administration, Sandy is a Consultant and Mentor to develop Leaders, Churches, and Businesses in Professional Development for Church/Ministry Excellence and Growth. Sandy is the mother of two adult children: a son Tyrone, daughter, Shondra, and the grandmother of five beautiful granddaughters. Sandy is also the

author of twenty-one successful inspirational/self-help books. Sandy is an active Board Member, Consultant, and Mentor for various leaders, Faith-Based

Grassroots Organizations and Ministries. Most important, she is ANOINTED and BROKEN to Teach/Preach the Gospel with POWER and AUTHORITY in Jesus' Name for such critical times as these!

Below are listed some of her education and training experiences, community education trainings and outreach services.
Building Better Families Counseling Services, Individual, Pre-Marriage, Dating, Family, Marriage, and Youth/Teen counseling, behavior and mental health assessments. Harris County Probation & Parole Department-Court Ordered Community Supervision Case Counseling, Texas Department of Criminal Justice Law Enforcement & Administration Professional Training, Texas Education for Secretaries Association (TESA) – Professional Development Training, Houston Police Department Cadet Training Academy – Domestic Violence Culture Sensitivity Training, Texas Institute Of Substance Abuse & Mental Health– Mental Health & Re-Entry Professionals Training, RayOliver's C.M.H.C - Chief Executive Officer, Administrator, Mental Health Assessment, Counseling, North Harris College Administration, Registration, Graduation, Financial Aid and Counseling, Rice University Administration, Registration, and Graduation.

Community & Professional Affiliations
The Texas Association Against Sexual Assault (TAASA)
The Bridge Women's Shelter
Strengthening Families Program
Family Wellness Associates
P.A.P.A. (Parenting & Paternity Awareness)
Building Better Families Behavior Wellness Services
Lifelong Learning Unlimited-Association For Community Education Credits
National Training Center for Recidivism Prevention
Texas Department of Criminal Justice Crime Victims Services
In His Loving Hands Ministry
Heart Two Heart Ministries
Elect Lady School Of Ministry
Woman Power Television Broadcast
WHOLE-Woman Books University
Beauty For Ashes Ministries, Inc.
PCS Publishing University
I-Flourish International Women's Ministry
SOAR Ministries
We Are More than Conquerors Ministries, Inc.
Solace Counseling Services
Think & Live Well Counseling Services
Family Time Counseling & Domestic Violence Shelter
Houston Area Women's Center
Ambassadors for the Holy Trinity Ministries, Inc.
Blessed Beyond Measure International Church
Christ Guide Counseling Center, Inc.

Dr. Sandy D. Murphy

Awards & Recognitions
Person Of The Week – Fox 26
People Who Make A Difference – Channels 13, 11, 2, 39, 55
International Who's Who of Women Entrepreneurs Award
Woman of Distinction Award-The Bridge Women's Center
Council Member At-Large Service Award- TDCJ Crime Victims Services
Media Services Interviews- Local/National Secular & Faith-based Radio, Television and Newspapers, TBN, Daystar, Sky Angel, Women Power Radio Show, KTSU, KYOK, KWWJ, KSBJ, KCHB, KRBE
Houston Mayor's Crime Victims Community Service Award
HPD Humanitarian Service Award
The AMIGOS Peace Award of Chicago
Multiple Community Service Appreciation Awards

Publications
Too Bad It Wasn't A Dream
Loosing The Persecuted Preacher-Woman
Why Lust Won't Let You Live
Inside-Out
The Cry of A Grass-widow's Child
How To Tell The "Don't Tell" Secrets Of Childhood Sexual Abuse
The Prayer & Praise Diary
His Journal Of Strength
My Living Testimony, "It" Get In The Blood
Freedom For Souls Tied To Devil Dream Lovers
Opening The Eyes Of Silly Women
The Top Ten Reasons Ministries Are Aborted & Churches Don't Grow
The Woman In The Rear View Mirror
Who Told You You're Gay?
Why I Can't Trust You
The Other Side of Covering Up & Coming Out of Gay/Lesbian Lifestyles
7~Iniquity Birth Marks That Shape Weak Men
Discerning Undercover SAP SUCKERS, A Spiritual "Fruit" Inspector Guide
Demons Are On Assignment, Who's Covering You?
Recognizing & Embracing Your Spiritual Mother, Mentor, Midwife
The Curse of DISHONOR
TRUST Recovery (*Past, Present, Future*) Session-I "What You DID & Didn't SAY

For Speaking Request, Workshops, Training, or Ministry/Leadership Equipping/Enrichment, Contact Dr. Murphy at:
P.O. Box 15211-Humble, Texas 77347
Direct Contact: (281) 372-0037, Email: eladysons@gmail.com
www.elected.webs.com

GET YOUR FREE BOOK!

Here's how to **INSTANTLY** receive

The above **FREE eBook** from

Dr. Murphy…….

Simply GO TO Amazon Books Online to SHARE

your **Personal BOOK REVIEW** Comments about

THIS BOOK: **Trust Recovery**

Please allow 3-4 Days for delivery.

Thanks for sharing your Reviews about this Book.

Talk to you soon in my NEXT Session with Sandy Series

NEED PERSONAL COUNSELING?

Dr. Sandy D. Murphy

Contact Dr. Murphy at:

Building Better Families, Inc.

Email: betterfamily3@gmail.com

OFFICE: (832)303-2451

P.O. Box 15211- Humble, Texas 77347

Website: www.buildbetterfamilies.webs.com

For Onsite Training Request

Email: elst12favor@gmail.com

www.ingramcontent.com/pod-product-compliance
Lightning Source LLC
Chambersburg PA
CBHW042024150426
43198CB00002B/60